★ *GREAT SPORTS TEAMS* ★

THE NEW YORK

YANKEES

BASEBALL TEAM

David Pietrusza

 Enslow Publishers, Inc.

44 Fadem Road	PO Box 38
Box 699	Aldershot
Springfield, NJ 07081	Hants GU12 6BP
USA	UK

Dedicated to Yankee fan Michael Chiara

Library of Congress Cataloging-in-Publication Data

Pietrusza, David, 1949–
    The New York Yankees baseball team / David Pietrusza.
       p. cm. — (Great sports teams)
    Includes bibliographical references and index.
    Summary: A team history of the most successful sports franchise of all time
focused on its greatest players and their legendary managers.
    ISBN 0-7660-1018-X
    1. New York Yankees (Baseball team)—History—Juvenile literature.
[1. New York Yankees (Baseball team)—History. 2. Baseball—History.]
I. Title. II. Series.
GV875.N4P54   1998
796.357′64′097471—dc21   97-19611
                                                        CIP
                                                            AC

Printed in the United States of America

10 9 8 7 6 5 4 3 2 1

Illustration Credits: AP/ Wide World Photos, pp. 4, 7, 8, 10, 13, 14, 16,
19, 20, 22, 25, 26, 28, 31, 32, 34, 37, 38.

Cover Illustration: AP/Wide World Photos.

CONTENTS

*W*rigley Field prior to the start of Game 3 of the 1932 World Series.

THE CALLED SHOT

I t was the grudge match to end all grudge matches. The year was 1932. The New York Yankees were at Wrigley Field playing the Chicago Cubs in the World Series. But it was more than a World Series; it was a personal grudge match between two highly talented teams.

Ready for a Fight

Yankee manager Joe McCarthy had led the Cubs to a pennant in 1929; they had fired him in 1930, and he immediately caught on with the New Yorkers. Infielder Mark Koenig, a former Yankee, had helped the Cubs to their 1932 pennant, batting .353 in 33 games. But his new Chicago teammates refused to give him a full World Series share. The Yankees stood up for their old friend, calling the Cubs cheapskates and worse—and the insults flew between the two benches, with the Cubs centering their own vicious insults on the Yankees' aging superstar Babe Ruth. Chicago fans joined in, showering the Babe with boos and catcalls. At the Yankees' team hotel, Cubs fans even spit at Ruth and his wife, Claire.

The Babe

There had never been a ballplayer like Ruth, and there never would be again. Raised in a Baltimore orphanage, he was a mountain of raw talent and raw emotion. He broke training rules, and he spent money as quickly as he took it in. In the Roaring Twenties, nobody roared louder than George Herman "Babe" Ruth. He began his major-league career as a very promising left-handed pitcher. Twice he won 20 games in a season. He set a record with 29 consecutive scoreless World Series innings. But he could also hit as no one had ever hit before. Before Ruth's arrival, baseball was a pitcher's game, but the Babe changed all that. In 1920 he slammed an amazing total of 54 homers. In 1921, he hit 59. In 1927, he broke that record when he hit 60. Fans flocked to see him wherever he played. They loved more than Ruth's slugging; they loved his exuberance, his flouting of authority, and his unique cheerful style. America loved the Babe.

It Only Takes One

Chicago in 1932 did not share that love. On October 1, nearly fifty thousand frenzied fans jammed Chicago's Wrigley Field to witness the Series' Game 3. It was all Cubs vs. Ruth. In the first inning the Bambino

*G*eorge Herman "Babe" Ruth of the New York Yankees crashes out his record-breaking home run number 60 on September 30, 1927, off Tom Zachary of the Washington Senators.

delivered a three-run homer, but in the fourth inning he missed a shoestring catch, and Chicago tied the score, 4-4. Ruth batted again in the top of the fifth. While he was waiting in the on-deck circle, a lemon had been thrown at him. As he took his place at the plate, a new chorus of boos and insults greeted him. The turmoil failed to faze the Babe. He smiled at the Cubs, who screamed insults at him. Then he calmly took Cubs right-hander Charlie Root's first offering for strike one. Ruth raised his right hand and held up his index finger. Then came two quick balls. Then another Root pitch cut the plate—for another called strike. Ruth stared at the hostile Cubs dugout. "It only

E *arle Combs was the Yankees center fielder from 1924–35. A member of the 1932 World Championship team, Combs was elected to the National Baseball Hall of Fame in 1970.*

takes one to hit it," he boasted, as he held up two fingers.[1]

Long Gone

Some said he had also pointed to center field, indicating that he would hit the next pitch there. Others said he did no such thing. But all agreed he had promised to hit Root's next offering for a homer. The right-hander's next pitch was over the plate. The Babe swung with all his might, and the ball went deep, deep to center field, deep into the Wrigley Field bleachers, deeper than any ball had gone before. It was his fifteenth World Series homer. "To me," the Babe later remembered, "it was the funniest, proudest moment I had ever had in baseball. I jogged down toward first base, rounded it, looked back at the Cub bench and suddenly convulsed with laughter."[2]

The mighty Bambino had done the impossible. He had called his shot in the World Series. His own legend was now complete, but the legend of baseball's greatest franchise, the New York Yankees, was just getting started.

Known as "Murderers' Row" the Yankees lineup terrorized opposing pitchers. Here are three of the main offenders: (left to right) Lou Gehrig, Babe Ruth, and Tony Lazzeri.

THE DYNASTIES

The New York Yankees and Babe Ruth had one very basic thing in common: Both were born in Baltimore.

When the American League started in 1901, it featured a franchise in Baltimore called the Orioles. But circuit president Ban Johnson knew that any successful major league would need to have a team in New York, the nation's largest city. So in 1903, the Baltimore Orioles became the New York Highlanders.

The Highlanders

The Highlanders played in upper Manhattan at tiny, ramshackle Hilltop Park. For the most part, they were not a very good team. It was only in 1913 that the club dropped its long name and became the Yankees. The next few years would see some dramatic changes for the team. New ownership arrived and began buying talent from other teams, primarily from the cash-strapped Boston Red Sox. The franchise moved from Hilltop Park into the bathtub-shaped Polo Grounds, the home of its National League rivals, the New York Giants.

Murderers' Row

The Yankees, led by Babe Ruth, won their first pennant in 1921 and their first world championship in 1923. The Yankees of the 1920s were a hard-hitting team, often called Murderers' Row. They reached their peak in 1927 when they won 110 regular season games and swept the Pittsburgh Pirates in that fall's World Series. Aiding Ruth in terrorizing league pitchers were first baseman Lou "The Iron Horse" Gehrig, second baseman Tony Lazzeri, and center fielder Earle Combs. Their slugging was dearly appreciated by New York hurlers. "A Yankee pitcher," joked one of them, Hall of Fame right-hander Waite Hoyt, "never should hold out, because he might be traded, and then he would have to pitch against them."[1]

The Yankees also moved into a new home, Yankee Stadium, the House That Ruth Built. No longer welcome at the Polo Grounds, the Yanks built their new field in the Bronx and became the Bronx Bombers. Opened on April 18, 1923, the huge Yankee Stadium became the most famous and fabled ballpark in baseball.

The Bronx Bombers

The Yankees of the 1930s may have been an even better team than the Murderers' Row clubs of the 1920s. Featuring Gehrig, center fielder Joe DiMaggio,

The New York Yankees Baseball Team

catcher Bill Dickey, and pitchers Red Ruffing and Lefty Gomez (all Hall of Famers), Joe McCarthy's Yanks won pennants in 1932, 1936, 1937, 1938, and 1939—and carried their good fortune into the 1940s, winning again in 1941, 1942, and 1943. Rooting for the Yanks, it was said, was like rooting for U.S. Steel; a large steel manufacturer that dominated the industry.

Stengel's Yankees

The Yankees paced the league again in 1947 but seemed about ready to run out of steam. In 1949, though, general manager George Weiss hired his old friend Casey Stengel to manage the club. Stengel's Yankees reeled off a record five-straight world championships. New Yankees stars included slick-fielding shortstop

*W*hitey Ford was the Yankees most dominant pitcher for most of the 1950s and 1960s. Ford holds the record for most World Series victories, 10.

Phil Rizzuto and savvy southpaw Whitey Ford. After losing the pennant to Cleveland in 1954, the Bronx Bombers came back to win four straight league flags and then another pennant in 1960. A highlight of the decade was right-hander Don Larsen's perfect game against the Brooklyn Dodgers in the 1956 World Series—the only perfect game in postseason history. "Playing with the Yankees was like a dream come true," marveled outfielder Gene Woodling.[2]

The Sixties

After Pittsburgh's dramatic last-minute victory over the Yanks in the 1960 World Series, the New York owners thought Weiss and Stengel were too old, and fired them. The Yankees still kept winning. In 1961, New York sluggers Mickey Mantle and Roger Maris both challenged Ruth's record for home runs in a season. Maris eventually won the competition, slamming 61 homers to Mantle's 54 as the Yanks posted 109 regular season wins and another world championship. But Maris could do more than hit homers. "He was a complete player," noted author Dom Forker. "He could hit, hit with power, drive home runs, field, throw strongly and accurately, run, take the extra base, go from first to third, take out the pivot man at second base—and bunt."[3] The club won pennants again in 1962, 1963, and 1964 under managers Ralph Houk and Yogi Berra, but a loud and sudden crash followed.

*B*eating the throw, Joe DiMaggio slides safely into home plate.

A GALAXY OF STARS

Since the days of Babe Ruth, the Yankees have featured many of baseball's greatest stars. The high-living Ruth hit 714 career home runs, drove in 2,213 runs, and sported a .342 lifetime batting average. He led the league twelve times in homers, six times in RBIs, and thirteen times in slugging. As a pitcher his career ERA was a glistening 2.28; his won-lost percentage was .671. Jumping Joe Dugan, a teammate of Ruth's, summed it up: "He wasn't human. No human could have done the things he did and lived the way he did and been a ballplayer. [Ty] Cobb? Could he pitch? [Tris] Speaker? The rest? I saw them. There was never anybody close."[1]

Lou Gehrig

First baseman Lou Gehrig was as quiet as Ruth was loud, and although he slammed 493 career homers, he was almost completely overshadowed by the boisterous Bambino. Larrupin' Lou was a steady, workmanlike player who overcame numerous injuries to play in a remarkable 2,130 consecutive games—a major-league record that survived until Baltimore's Cal Ripken, Jr. shattered it in 1995.

Sadly, only the specter of death could force the sturdy Gehrig out of the lineup. He contracted amyotrophic lateral sclerosis (ALS, also called Lou Gehrig's Disease), which led to his death in 1941. When it came time for him to leave the Yankees in 1939, he departed with great dignity and courage, telling 61,808 fans at Yankee Stadium: "I consider myself the luckiest man on the face of the earth."[2]

Joe DiMaggio

Center fielder Joe DiMaggio, the Yankee Clipper, was nearly as quiet as Lou Gehrig, but possessed an element of grace and dignity that set him apart from other ballplayers. Gliding across Yankee Stadium's vast center field, Joltin' Joe made it look easy, even though he always gave it his best. "There might be a kid in the stands, or five kids or ten, who had never seen me play or would never see me play again," he once told a friend. "I burned to be the best there was for them, to leave them with a good memory of me."[3]

Like Gehrig, DiMaggio achieved one of baseball's most remarkable streaks—his 56-game hitting streak in 1941. After the Indians' third baseman, Ken Keltner, stopped DiMaggio's streak with two sensational plays, Joltin' Joe hit safely again the next day, and continued hitting safely for 16 more games. Three times

The New York Yankees Baseball Team

O ne of the all-time greats, Mickey Mantle won three Most Valuable Player awards, 1956, 1957, and 1962.

he won the MVP Award. In 1949 he became the first player to earn a $100,000 salary.

Mickey Mantle

When it came time for DiMaggio to retire, the Yankees had another superstar center fielder to replace him—Mickey Mantle. The Oklahoma-born Mantle combined awesome power and blinding speed and may have been the most dominating player of the 1950s. He was, however, injury-prone, and he played most of his career in pain. The Mick was known for his "tape-measure" home runs. Perhaps his most famous home

*R*eggie Jackson admires another one of his home run blasts. Jackson was one of the most exciting ballplayers of the 1970s and 1980s.

run traveled 565 feet at Washington's Griffith Stadium in 1953. On May 13, 1955, he collected three homers, all hit into Yankee Stadium's bleachers. Each blast cleared the 461-foot sign. On May 22, 1963, a Mantle blast struck Yankee Stadium's high right-field facade. Experts calculated that had the homer kept sailing, it would have traveled 620 feet.

Reggie Jackson

Reggie Jackson was a throwback to the colorful Ruth. Noted for his power and his postseason clutch hitting (which earned him the nickname Mr. October), Jackson may have been the brashest Yankee ever to wear pinstripes. He feuded with teammates, owner George Steinbrenner, and manager Billy Martin, but the controversy could not keep him from hitting 563 homers. When the egotistical Jackson bragged he was so good, they would name a candy bar after him, teammate Catfish Hunter shot back, "When you unwrap a Reggie bar, it tells you how good it is."[4]

In 1993, the Hall of Fame told Reggie how good he was, electing him to Cooperstown the first year he was on the ballot.

*J*oe McCarthy anxiously awaits the start of the
1932 World Series. McCarthy managed the
Yanks from 1931–46.

WINNING LEADERSHIP

The New York Yankees have not only featured many of the national pastime's greatest players, they have also boasted some of the game's brainiest managers.

Miller Huggins

The Murderers' Row teams of the 1920s were led by a mighty mite, Miller Huggins. Just 5 feet 6-1/2 inches and 140 pounds, the former Cardinals infielder and law school graduate had his hands full dealing with Ruth and his uproarious teammates. In 1925, Huggins had to fine Ruth $5,000—a substantial sum, considering that Ruth, then by far the game's best-paid player, was earning only $52,000 per year. Despite—or perhaps because of—such incidents, Huggins led the Yankees to six pennants in eight years. In the middle of the 1929 season, Huggins, just fifty, tragically died of blood poisoning.

Joe McCarthy

Joe McCarthy was known as the Yanks' "push-button manager" because it was said that with the talent the Yankees possessed, McCarthy could just push a button and they would win. McCarthy had never played even one game in the majors, and when he first came to manage in the big leagues, he had to prove he was no busher. He did that when he won the pennant in 1929 with the Cubs, then revived a slumping Yankees franchise. From 1936 through 1939, McCarthy's Yanks won four straight world championships. Then they won pennants again in 1941, 1942, and 1943. Few managers ever pushed buttons as well as Marse Joe, and he did it with class. McCarthy believed in strict professionalism and a Yankees code of conduct. "He would never say anything behind a player's back," remembered shortstop Phil Rizzuto, "and he would never second-guess his men."[1]

Casey Stengel

Casey "The Old Perfesser" Stengel had a reputation as a double-talking clown when he joined the Yankees in 1949. Once, as a player, when he had doffed his cap to the crowd, a sparrow flew out. But worse than that, he had failed to produce winners while managing the Braves and Dodgers. Many thought GM George Weiss had taken leave of his senses in hiring his old friend. But Stengel made believers out of his critics after breaking McCarthy's record by registering five straight world championships. The key to Stengel's success

The New York Yankees Baseball Team

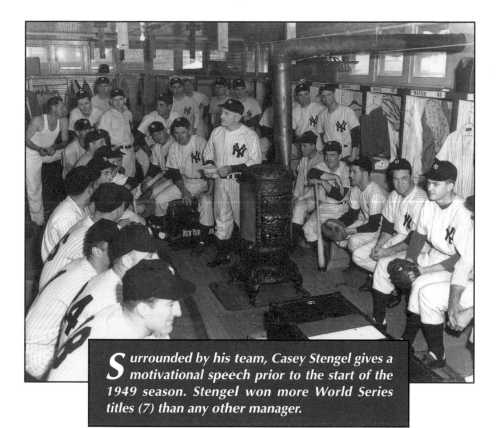

*S*urrounded by his team, Casey Stengel gives a motivational speech prior to the start of the 1949 season. Stengel won more World Series titles (7) than any other manager.

was his unique style of platooning players, using them only in situations in which they would do their best. "Stengel," noted author Ed Linn, "showed that the bench and the bullpen were just as important as the starting lineup. He demonstrated how games could be won by protecting good hitters from pitchers who could exploit their one weakness, and by choosing the one best spot to exploit a weaker hitter's strength."[2]

Stengel was also smart enough to know that not every player was happy being platooned. "The secret to managing," he would say, "is to keep the guys who hate you from the guys who are undecided."[3]

Yankees manager Billy Martin argues a call with umpire Jim Evans. In the late 1970s Martin helped turn the Yankees back into championship contenders.

Billy Martin

One of the Old Perfesser's prize pupils was infielder Billy Martin. Fifteen years after the Yanks fired Stengel, the scrappy Martin—after stints managing the Twins, Tigers, and Rangers—became the Yankees manager, and the center of baseball's most sensational soap opera. Gone were the days of Yankee dignity, and pennants. They had not been in the World Series since 1964. Martin didn't just have to battle rival American League teams; he also had to battle controversial Yankees owner George Steinbrenner. Five times Steinbrenner hired him, and five times Steinbrenner fired him.

The Martin era would be noisy, but it returned the World Series back to the House That Ruth Built. "Billy Martin," observed Boston's Carl Yastrzemski, "has had the ability to take mediocre teams and make them good; now he has taken a good team and made it great."[4]

R on Guidry jokes around with Yankees owner
George Steinbrenner. Guidry was a 20 game
winner three times for the Yankees, and won the
A.L. Cy Young Award in 1978.

THE BRONX ZOO

n 1976, the Billy Martin–led Yankees ended an eleven-year drought and captured the league pennant, the first of three straight flags. New stars—Reggie Jackson, catcher Thurman Munson, third baseman Graig Nettles, pitchers Ron "Louisiana Lightning" Guidry, Jim "Catfish" Hunter, and reliever Sparky Lyle—arrived. But in the process, the old respectable push-button Yankees disappeared. A new form of Yankee team emerged at the Yankee Stadium: the Bronx Zoo.

These new Yankees fought with each other, with Billy Martin, and with owner Steinbrenner. "When I was a kid, I wanted to play baseball and join the circus," joked Graig Nettles. "With the Yankees, I've been able to do both."[1]

Back in Contention

The Yankees won the American League East in 1976, and faced the Kansas City Royals in a hard-fought

American League Championship Series (ALCS). That series went down to the wire. In the pivotal Game 5, the Royals' George Brett hit an eighth-inning three-run homer to tie the game. Then Yankees first baseman Chris Chambliss homered in the bottom of the ninth to give the Bronx Bombers the pennant. In the World Series, however, the Yanks were swept by Cincinnati's Big Red Machine. This infuriated George Steinbrenner, who responded by signing free agent Reggie Jackson. The move paid off. The Bronx Bombers won the pennant again in 1977, in that fall's World Series against the Dodgers, and Jackson established his reputation as Mr. October by slamming a record three homers in Game 6.

Munson vs. Jackson

This team also was marked by misfortune. Reggie Jackson and hard-nosed catcher Thurman Munson had battled for team leadership. "I'm the straw that stirs the drink," Jackson once boasted. "It all comes back to me. Maybe I should say me and Munson. But he really doesn't enter into it. He can only stir it bad."[2] Yet the two players both had their roles to play in the club's success. Munson, however, was soon to die a tragic death. On August 2, 1979, his private plane crashed as he was returning home. His two passengers survived, but Munson was killed.

In-between Years

The 1978 American League pennant race was among the greatest ever. By July 19, the Yankees were 14 games

The New York Yankees Baseball Team

*T*hurman Munson was an all-star player and a
team leader for the Yankees in the 1970s.

behind their hated rivals, the Boston Red Sox. Then the
Yankees battled back. By early September, New York
held a 3½ game lead. Now it was Boston's turn to
scramble. By season's end, they had caught the Yanks,
ending the season in a tie for first. The pennant hung
on a special one-game tie-breaker. The Yanks seemed
on the verge of defeat until an unlikely hero emerged:
New York's normally light-hitting shortstop, Bucky
Dent. In the seventh inning, Dent hit a windblown fly
ball that carried over Fenway Park's Green Monster. It
went for a three-run homer and gave the Yanks a lead
they never surrendered—and the pennant.

The Yankees won the A.L. East in 1980 (but lost the
ALCS to Kansas City) and the pennant in 1981. After

*D*on Mattingly (right) receives congratulations from teammate Mel Hall (27) after launching a homer. One of the most popular Yankees, Mattingly won the 1985 A.L. MVP.

taking the first two Series games against the Dodgers, however, the Yanks were swept in four straight contests.

The Long Drought

That began another long Series drought. Despite stars such as first baseman Don Mattingly, second baseman Willie Randolph, and speedy outfielder Rickey Henderson, the Yankees of the 1980s never again reached the postseason. For most of the decade, the once-invincible Yankees were overshadowed by the once-downtrodden Mets.

In 1994, the club finally seemed pennant bound again, but it was cheated out of World Series glory by that season's strike, which canceled the postseason. The following year, New York finally made it, although it took the new wild card format for the Yankees to do it. Manager Buck Showalter's team faced the upstart Seattle Mariners in the first round of the postseason, and a truly exciting series resulted, but Seattle prevailed in five games. New York would have to wait until the next year.

David Cone joined the Yankees in a 1995 trade with the Toronto Blue Jays. Cone was the A.L. Cy Young Award winner in 1994 as a member of the Kansas City Royals.

"BEST TEAM FOR '96"

At the end of the 1995 season, Yanks manager Buck Showalter resigned. George Steinbrenner once again went looking for a new manager and found one in former Mets, Braves, and Cardinals pilot Joe Torre.

A Talented Team

Torre's 1996 Yankees started the season with an intriguing mix of old and new talent. Veterans included third baseman Wade Boggs; outfielder Tim Raines; first baseman Tino Martinez; starting pitchers David Cone, Kenny Rogers, Jimmy Key, and Dwight Gooden; and bullpen ace John Wetteland. Youngsters included sophomore starter Andy Pettitte, rookie shortstop Derek Jeter, center fielder Bernie Williams, and middle reliever Mariano Rivera.

The Yankees got off to an excellent start, at one time holding a 12½ game lead over second-place

Baltimore. Dwight Gooden confounded his critics by no-hitting Seattle in May. This new type of Yankees team was built on pitching and defense, and it lacked the power of previous Yankees champions. So Steinbrenner went out and acquired two genuine sluggers: Detroit first baseman Cecil Fielder and former Mets star Darryl Strawberry. The troubled Strawberry was playing in an independent minor league, the Northern League, when the Yankees signed him in July.

Some Problems Arise

Steinbrenner's strategy did not seem to pay off. New York's lead dwindled to just 2fi games. David Cone left the starting rotation with an aneurysm in his right shoulder. Gooden also ran out of gas. But the Yankees battled back. On September 3, Cone returned. In his first start, he pitched seven no-hit innings against the Oakland A's. The Yankees held on to beat Baltimore in the A.L. East division by four games.

A Little Luck

The Yankees rolled over the A.L. West Division champion Texas Rangers in the postseason's first round, then faced wild card Baltimore in the ALCS. In Game 1, the Yankees received unexpected help from a twelve-year-old fan. Jeffrey Maier caught a fair fly ball hit by Derek Jeter. Instead of calling Jeter out for fan interference, umpires credited him with a homer crucial to the Yankees' win. It took only four more games for New York to defeat Baltimore. Key to the

*R*ookie shortstop Derek Jeter was a major part of the Yankees' success in 1996. Jeter won the American League's Rookie of the Year Award for his efforts.

triumph was Strawberry, who slammed three homers and batted .417. "Playing in the Northern League showed I cared about the game and wanted to return," said Strawberry, "but I wanted to return in a very positive way."[1]

The Yankees, however, looked clearly over-matched when the World Series opened against

*A*ndy Pettitte celebrates after the Yankees' 1996 World Series victory. Pettitte won over twenty games in only his second season in the major leagues.

Atlanta. In Game 1, the Braves erupted with a 12-1 win. They won Game 2, 4-0. It looked like it was all over for the Yanks. "We embarrassed ourselves the first two games in New York," admitted Yankees catcher Joe Girardi. "Whatever was written about us was well deserved because we stunk."[2]

A Turn for the Better

New York bounced back, traveling to Atlanta and sweeping the three games played at Atlanta–Fulton County Stadium. Games 4 and 5 were particularly thrilling. Game 4 saw the Yankees down 6-0, but they battled back to tie it on catcher Jim Leyritz's three-run homer before winning, 8-6, in ten innings. Game 5 saw New York win, 1-0, behind the gutsy pitching of Pettitte and Wetteland and right fielder Paul O'Neill's limping grab to end the game.

The Braves, with Greg Maddux pitching, should have won Game 6 but didn't. Instead, New York held on to win, 3-2, and wrapped up its twenty-third World Series win. The victory was particularly sweet for manager Joe Torre, whose brother, Frank, had received a long-awaited heart transplant the day before.

"People didn't see the Yankees in the first two games," said Torre. "These last four games . . . these were the real Yankees."[3]

The Yankees knew they had beaten a quality opponent. "They're the team of the '90s," said Bernie Williams about Atlanta, "but we're the best team for '96."[4]

STATISTICS

Team Record

The Yankees History

YEARS	LOCATION	W	L	PCT.	PENNANTS	WORLD SERIES
1901–09	Baltimore (1901–03) New York	638	671	.487	None	None
1910–19	New York	701	780	.473	None	None
1920–29	New York	933	602	.608	1921–23, 1926–28	1923, 1927–28
1930–39	New York	970	554	.636	1932, 1936–39	1932, 1936–39
1940–49	New York	929	609	.604	1941–43 1947, 1949	1941, 1943 1947, 1949
1950–59	New York	955	582	.621	1950–53, 1955–58	1950–53, 1956, 1958
1960–69	New York	887	720	.552	1960–64	1961–62
1970–79	New York	892	715	.555	1976–78	1977–78
1980–89	New York	854	708	.547	1981	None
1990–96	New York	543	524	.509	1996	1996

The Yankees Today

YEAR	W	L	PCT.	COACH	DIVISION FINISH
1990	67	95	.414	Bucky Dent Stump Merrill	7
1991	71	91	.438	Stump Merrill	5
1992	76	86	.469	Buck Showalter	4 (tie)
1993	88	74	.543	Buck Showalter	2
1994	70	43	.619	Buck Showalter	1

The Yankees Today (con't)

YEAR	W	L	PCT.	COACH	DIVISION FINISH
1995	79	65	.549	Buck Showalter	2
1996	92	70	.568	Joe Torre	1

Total History

W	L	PCT.	PENNANTS	WORLD SERIES
8,302	6,465	.562	35	23

W=Wins
L=Losses
PCT.=Winning Percentage

PENNANTS=Won league title.
WORLD SERIES=Won World Series.

Championship Managers

COACH	YEARS COACHED	RECORD	WORLD CHAMPIONSHIPS
Miller Huggins	1918–29	1,067-719	1923, 1927–28
Joe McCarthy	1931–46	1,460-867	1932, 1936–39, 1941, 1943
Bucky Harris	1947–48	191-117	1947
Casey Stengel	1949–60	1,149-696	1949–53, 1956, 1958
Ralph Houk	1961–63 1966–73	944-816	1961–62
Billy Martin	1975–78 1979, 1983 1985, 1988	556-385	1977
Bob Lemon	1978–79 1981–82	99-71	1978
Joe Torre	1996–	92-70	1996

Great Hitters

PLAYER	SEA	YRS	G	AB	R	H	HR	RBI	SB	AVG
Yogi Berra	1946–63	19	2,120	7,555	1,175	2,150	358	1,430	30	.285
Joe DiMaggio	1936–42	13	1,736	6,821	1,390	2,214	361	1,537	30	.325
Lou Gehrig	1923–39	17	2,164	8,001	1,888	2,721	493	1,995	102	.340
Reggie Jackson	1977–81	21	2,820	9,864	1,551	2,584	563	1,702	228	.262
Derek Jeter	1995–	2	172	630	109	195	10	85	14	.310
Mickey Mantle	1951–68	18	2,401	8,102	1,677	2,415	536	1,509	153	.298
Tino Martinez	1996–	7	698	2,491	332	676	113	429	5	.271
Don Mattingly	1982–95	14	1,785	7,003	1,007	2,153	222	1,099	13	.307
Babe Ruth	1920–34	22	2,503	8,399	2,174	2,873	714	2,213	123	.342
Bernie Williams	1991–	6	681	2,670	430	760	79	369	67	.285

SEA=Seasons with Yankees
YRS=Years in the Majors
G=Games
AB=At Bats

R=Runs Scored
H=Hits
HR=Home Runs
RBI=Runs Batted In

SB=Stolen Bases
AVG=Batting Average

Great Pitchers

PLAYER	SEA	YRS	W	L	PCT	ERA	G	SV	IP	K	SH
David Cone	1995–	11	136	80	.630	3.16	299	1	1,994	1,812	21
Whitey Ford	1950–67	16	236	106	.690	2.75	498	10	3,170	1,956	45
Goose Gossage	1978–83, 1989	22	124	107	.537	3.01	1,002	310	1,809	1,502	0
Waite Hoyt	1921–30	21	237	182	.566	3.59	674	52	3,762	1,206	26
Andy Pettitte	1995–	2	33	17	.660	4.00	66	0	396	276	0

SEA=Seasons with Yankees
YRS=Years in the Majors
W=Wins
L=Losses

PCT=Winning Percentage
ERA=Earned Run Average
G=Games
SV=Saves

IP=Innings Pitched
K=Strikeouts
SH=Shutouts

The New York Yankees Baseball Team

CHAPTER NOTES

Chapter 1

1. Robert W. Creamer, *Babe* (New York: Simon & Schuster, 1976), p. 363.

2. Babe Ruth, *The Babe Ruth Story* (Winston-Salem, N.C.: Starbooks, 1948), p. 195.

Chapter 2

1. Paul Dickson, *Baseball's Greatest Quotations* (New York: HarperCollins, 1991), p. 191.

2. Dom Forker, *The Men of Autumn* (Dallas: Taylor, 1989), p. 178.

3. Dom Forker, *Sweet Seasons* (Dallas: Taylor, 1990), pp. 188–189.

Chapter 3

1. John Mosedale, *The Greatest of All: The 1927 New York Yankees* (New York: Dial, 1974), p. 158.

2. John Thorn, Pete Palmer, Michael Gershman, and David Pietrusza, eds. *Total Baseball* (New York: Viking, 1997), p. 166.

3. Maury Allen, *Where Have You Gone, Joe DiMaggio?* (New York: Dutton, 1975), p. 191.

4. Bob Chieger, *Voices of Baseball* (New York: Signet, 1983), p. 135.

Chapter 4

1. Lowell Reidenbaugh, *Cooperstown* (New York: Crescent, 1993), p. 198.

2. Robert W. Creamer, *Stengel: His Life and Times* (New York: Simon & Schuster, 1984), p. 252.

3. Paul Dickson, *Baseball's Greatest Quotations* (New York: HarperCollins, 1991), p. 424.

4. David Falkner, *The Last Yankee* (New York: Simon & Schuster, 1992), p. 214.

Chapter 5

1. Bob Chieger, ed., *Voices of Baseball* (New York: Signet, 1983), p. 37.

2. Reggie Jackson with Mike Lupica, *Reggie* (New York: Ballantine, 1984), p. 144.

Chapter 6

1. Deron Snyder, "The Yankees' Leading Man," *USA Today Baseball Weekly*, October 16–22, 1996, p. 28.

2. Ben Walker, "Yankees Seek to Wrap Up Title," *Albany Times Union*, October 26, 1996, p. C-1.

3. Jim Salisbury, "Yanks on Top of the World: Finish Off the Braves for 23rd Series Title," *New York Post*, October 26, 1996.

4. Ibid.

GLOSSARY

American League—One of the two major leagues of baseball, founded in 1901 by Ban Johnson. The other major league is the National League, founded in 1876. The primary difference between the two leagues is that since 1973 the American League (AL) has used the designated hitter rule.

amyotrophic lateral sclerosis (ALS, or Lou Gehrig's Disease)—A rare progressive degenerative fatal disease, usually starting in middle age, affecting the spinal cord, and characterized by increasing muscular weakness.

aneurysm—An abnormal blood-filled dilatation of a blood vessel, especially an artery, resulting from disease of the vessel wall.

batting average—At bats divided by hits.

"Big Red Machine"—The great Cincinnati Reds teams of the mid-1970s. They captured world championships in 1975 and 1976.

bunt—A batted ball that is tapped softly in the infield; a bunt may be used either for a base hit or to advance a runner.

busher—Someone whose career is spent in the minor leagues, also known as the bush leagues.

Cy Young Award—Award given each year to the best pitcher in each major league; named after Hall of Fame pitcher Cy Young.

designated hitter—A player who does not take the field during the game, but only bats. In the major leagues, the designated hitter (DH) is used only in the American League.

ERA (Earned Run Average)—The number of earned runs divided by the number of innings pitched times nine. The ERA is perhaps the best measure of pitching effectiveness.

fly ball—A ball hit in the air, as opposed to a ground ball.

free agent—A major leaguer whose contractual obligations to his old team have expired and who is free to sign with any major-league team.

holdout—A player who wants a larger salary and does not return his contract for the upcoming season.

Hall of Fame—Located in Cooperstown, N.Y., membership in the National Baseball Hall of Fame is the highest honor that can be awarded to a professional player.

homer—A home run.

House That Ruth Built—A nickname for Yankee Stadium.

infielder—Someone who plays an infield position (first, second, or third base, or shortstop).

League Championship Series (LCS)—The best-of-seven series that determines the American and National League champions.

MVP Award—Most Valuable Player Award.

pennant—A league championship, also called the flag.

pivot man—The relay player at second base during a double play.

platooning—Alternating players at a given position to take advantage of their strengths, usually taking into consideration whether they are left- or right-handed hitters.

RBI—A run batted in.

Rookie of the Year Award—Award given each year to the best rookie (or new major league player) in each major league.

rotator cuff—A supporting portion of the shoulder. A torn rotator cuff can seriously damage a pitcher's effectiveness and jeopardize his career.

southpaw—A left-handed person.

wild card—The nondivision winning club with the best won-lost percentage in regular season play. The wild card team in each league earns a chance for postseason play.

World Series—The end of the season best-of-seven series that pits the champions of the National and American leagues against each other.

FURTHER READING

Allen, Maury. *Where Have You Gone, Joe DiMaggio?* New York: Dutton, 1975.

Chieger, Bob. *Voices of Baseball.* New York: Signet, 1983.

Creamer, Robert W. *Babe.* New York: Simon & Schuster, 1976.

————. *Stengel: His Life and Times.* New York: Simon and Schuster, 1984.

Deane, Bill. *Top 10 Baseball Hitters.* Springfield, N.J.: Enslow Publishers, Inc., 1998.

————. *Top 10 Baseball Home Run Hitters.* Springfield, N.J.: Enslow Publishers, Inc., 1997.

Dickson, Paul. *Baseball's Greatest Quotations.* New York: HarperCollins, 1991.

Falkner, David. *The Last Yankee.* New York: Simon and Schuster, 1992.

Forker, Dom. *The Men of Autumn.* Dallas: Taylor, 1989.

————. *Sweet Seasons.* Dallas: Taylor, 1990.

Jackson, Reggie, with Mike Lupica. *Reggie.* New York: Ballantine, 1984.

Mosedale, John. *The Greatest of All: The 1927 New York Yankees.* New York: Dial, 1974.

Reidenbaugh, Lowell. *Cooperstown.* New York: Crescent, 1993.

Ruth, Babe. *The Babe Ruth Story.* Winston-Salem, N.C.: Starbooks, 1948.

Thorn, John, Pete Palmer, Michael Gershman, and David Pietrusza, eds. *Total Baseball.* Fifth edition. New York: Viking, 1997.

The New York Yankees Baseball Team

INDEX

WHERE TO WRITE

New York Yankees
Yankee Stadium
Bronx, NY 10451

WEBSITE
http://www.yankees.com